To

_____

From

_____

Little Book

DEVOTIONS
31 DAILY DEVOTIONALS

Self-control

Little Book

DEVOTIONS

Self-control

The quoted ideas expressed in this book (but not scripture verses) are not, in all cases, exact quotations, as some have been edited for clarity and brevity. In all cases, the author has attempted to maintain the speaker's original intent. In some cases, quoted material for this book was obtained from secondary sources, primarily print media. While every effort was made to ensure the accuracy of these sources, the accuracy cannot be guaranteed. For additions, deletions, corrections or clarifications in future editions of this text, please write BRIGHTON BOOKS.

The Holy Bible, King James Version

The Holy Bible, New King James Version (NKJV) Copyright © 1982 by Thomas Nelson, Inc. Used by permission.

New Century Version®. (NCV) Copyright © 1987, 1988, 1991 by Word Publishing, a division of Thomas Nelson, Inc. All rights reserved. Used by permission.

International Children's Bible®, New Century Version®. (ICB) Copyright © 1986, 1988, 1999 by Tommy Nelson™, a division of Thomas Nelson, Inc. All rights reserved. Used by permission.

The Holman Christian Standard Bible™ (HCSB) Copyright © 1999, 2000, 2001 by Holman Bible Publishers. Used by permission.

The prayers and essays in this book are written by Criswell Freeman; used with permission.

Compiled and Edited: Mary Susan Freeman
Cover Design: Kim Russel, Wahoo Designs
Page Layout: Bart Dawson

ISBN 1-58334-222-2

Printed in the United States of America

For All of God's Children

Table of Contents

A Message to Parents

The fact that you've picked up this book proves that you're a thoughtful parent who is interested in both the spiritual and intellectual development of your child. Congratulations!

This text is intended to be read by Christian parents to their young children. The book contains 31 brief chapters, one for each day of the month. Each chapter is composed of a Bible verse, a brief story, helpful hints for kids and for parents, and a prayer. Every chapter examines some aspect of an important Biblical theme: self-control.

For the next 31 days, try this experiment: read one chapter each night to your child, and then spend a few more moments talking about the chapter's meaning. By the end of the month, you will have had 31 different opportunities to share God's wisdom with your son or daughter, and that's a very good thing.

You know how God's love has refashioned your own life. Now it's your turn to share your Heavenly Father's Good News with the boy or girl whom He has entrusted to your care. Happy reading! And may God continue to bless you and yours, now and forever.

Self-control

1

Self-control Means Looking before You Leap

Trust the Lord with all your heart.
Don't depend on your own understanding.
Remember the LORD in everything you do.
And he will give you success.

❋ ❋ ❋

Proverbs 3:5-6 ICB

Maybe you've heard this old saying: "Look before you leap." What does that saying mean? It means that you should stop and think before you do something. Otherwise, you might be sorry you did it.

Learning how to control yourself is an important part of growing up. The more you learn about self-control, the better. Self-control will help you at home, at school, and at church. That's why parents and teachers are happy to talk about the rewards of good self-control. And that's why you should be excited about learning how important it is to look before you leap . . . not after!

Think ahead: Before you do something, ask yourself this question: "Will I be ashamed if my parents find out?" If the answer to that question is "Yes," don't do it!

WOW
The alternative to discipline is disaster.
Vance Havner

Wait patiently for your child to grow up. Some bad habits, like impulsive behavior and temper tantrums, are simply a sign of youthful immaturity. If you maintain a steady hand, a loving heart, and a level head, this troubling behavior will, in all likelihood, subside as your child matures.

Dear Lord,
sometimes I make mistakes.
When I do, forgive me.
And help me, Lord, to learn
from my mistakes so that
I can be a better person
and a better example
to my friends and family.

Amen

2 Patience Please!

Always be humble and gentle. Be patient and accept each other with love.

Ephesians 4:2 ICB

Do you want to learn self-control? Then you must learn the art of being patient. The dictionary defines the word *patience* as "the ability to be calm, tolerant, and understanding." Here's what that means: the word *calm* means being in control of your emotions (not letting your emotions control you). The word *tolerant* means being kind and considerate to people who are different from you. And, the word *understanding* means being able to put yourself in another person's shoes.

If you can be calm, tolerant, and understanding, you will be the kind of person whose good deeds are a blessing to your family and friends. And that's exactly the kind of person that God wants you to be.

KiD TiP

What's good for you is good for them, too: If you want others to be patient with you, then you should treat them in the same way. That's the Golden Rule, and it should be your rule, too!

WOW
God is more patient with us
than we are with ourselves.
Max Lucado

Parent Tip

They learn by watching: Kids imitate their parents, so act accordingly! The best way for your child to learn to be patient is by example . . . your example!

Dear Lord,
sometimes I am not very patient.
Slow me down and calm me down.
Help me to think wisely and
to act wisely. Today and
every day, help me to learn
the wisdom of patience.

Amen

3

When the Teacher Isn't Looking

The honest person will live safely, but
the one who is dishonest will be caught.

❋❋❋

Proverbs 10:9 ICB

When your teachers or parents aren't watching, what should you do? The answer, of course, is that you should behave exactly like you would if they were watching you. But sometimes, you may be tempted to do otherwise.

When a parent steps away or a teacher looks away, you may be tempted to say something or do something that you would not do if they were standing right beside you. But remember this: when nobody's watching, it's up to you to control yourself. And that's exactly what everybody wants you to do: your teachers want you to control yourself, and so do your parents. And so, by the way, does God.

Behavior you can be proud of: When teachers or parents aren't looking, it's up to you to control yourself. So think about what you're doing, and think about the consequences of your behavior.

WOW
The single most important element
in any human relationship is honesty—
with oneself, with God, and with others.
Catherine Marshall

Self-control at school starts at home: Teachers can certainly help, but we cannot expect them to retrain our children. When it comes to the importance of self-control, we, as parents, must be the ones to teach our kids how to behave.

Dear Lord,
sometimes it's easier to
misbehave than it is to slow down
and think about the best way
to behave. But even when
doing the right thing is difficult,
let me slow down long enough
to think about the right thing
to say or do.

Amen

Listen to Your Conscience

4

They show that in their hearts
they know what is right and wrong.

Romans 2:15 ICB

God gave you something called a conscience: some people describe it as a little voice, but really, it's a feeling—it's a feeling that tells you whether something is right or wrong. Your conscience will usually tell you what to do and when to do it. Pay attention to that feeling, and trust it.

If you slow down and listen to your conscience, you'll usually stay out of trouble. And if you listen to your conscience, it won't be so hard to control your own behavior. Why? Because most of the time, your conscience already knows right from wrong. So don't be in such a hurry to do things. Instead of "jumping right in," listen to your conscience. In the end, you'll be very glad you did.

If you're not sure what to do . . . trust your conscience. It's almost always right!

WOW
God has revealed Himself in
a person's conscience. Conscience has been
described as the light of the soul.
Billy Graham

Where should they learn right from wrong? When it comes to teaching Christian values to our children, home school is always in session. Preach, teach, and behave accordingly.

Dear Lord,
You have given me a conscience
that tells me what is right and
what is wrong. I will listen to
that quiet voice so I can do the
right thing today and every day.

Amen

The Golden Rule

5

This royal law is found in the Scriptures:
"Love your neighbor as yourself."
If you obey this law, then
you are doing right.

James 2:8 ICB

When we learn how to control ourselves, we can be more considerate of other people. Would you like to make the world a better place? If so, you can start by practicing the Golden Rule.

Jesus said, "Do to others what you want them to do to you" (Matthew 7: 12 NCV). That means that you should treat other people in the very same way that you want to be treated. That's the Golden Rule.

Jesus wants us to treat other people with respect, kindness, courtesy, and love. When we do, we make our families and friends happy . . . and we make our Father in heaven very proud. So if you want to know how to treat other people, ask the person you see every time you look into the mirror. The answer you receive will tell you exactly what to do.

How would you feel? When you're trying to decide how to treat another person, ask yourself this question: "How would I feel if somebody treated me that way?" Then, treat the other person the way that you would want to be treated.

WOW
The Golden Rule starts at home, but it should never stop there.

Marie T. Freeman

Parent Tip

Words are never enough: When it comes to teaching our children the most important lessons, the things we say pale in comparison to the things we do. Being a responsible parent is a big job, but don't fret: you and God, working together, can handle it!

Dear Lord,
help me always to do my very
best to treat others as
I wish to be treated.
The Golden Rule is Your rule,
Father; let me also make it mine.

Amen

6

Learning to Wait Your Turn

Patience is better than strength.

Proverbs 16:32 ICB

When we're standing in line or waiting our turn, it's tempting to push ahead of other people. And it's tempting to scream, "Me first!", but it's the wrong thing to do! The Bible tells us that we shouldn't push ahead of others; instead, we should do the right thing—and the polite thing—by saying, "You first!"

Sometimes, waiting your turn can be hard, especially if you're excited or in a hurry. But even then, waiting patiently is the right thing to do. Why? Because parents say so, teachers say so, and, most importantly, God says so!

God and your parents have been patient with you . . . now it's your turn to be patient with others.

WOW
If only we could be as patient
with other people as God is with us!
Jim Gallery

Parent Tip

Be patient with your child's impatience: Children are supposed to be more impulsive than adults; after all, they're still kids. So be understanding of your child's limitations and understanding of his or her imperfections.

Dear Lord,
sometimes it's hard to be
a patient person, and that's
exactly when I should try my
hardest to be patient. Help me
to be patient and kind,
even when it's hard.

Amen

7

Following Directions

In all your ways acknowledge Him,
and He shall direct your paths.

Proverbs 3:6 NKJV

Directions, directions, directions. It seems like somebody is always giving you directions: telling you where to go, how to behave, and what to do next. But sometimes all these directions can be confusing! How can you understand everything that everybody tells you? The answer, of course, is that you must pay careful attention to those directions . . . and that means listening.

To become a careful listener, here are some things you must do:

1. Don't talk when you're supposed to be listening (your ears work best when your mouth is closed);

2. Watch the person who's giving the directions (when your eyes and ears work together, it's easier to understand things);

3. If you don't understand something, ask a question (it's better to ask now than to make a mistake later).

If you're afraid to raise your hand and ask a question, remember this . . . if you don't understand something, lots of other people in the classroom probably don't understand it, either. So you'll be doing everybody a big favor if you raise your hand and ask your question.

WOW
Obey God one step at a time,
then the next step will come into view.
Catherine Marshall

Giving directions? Here are a few tips: Be friendly; speak slowly; encourage lots of questions; give lots of examples; say it in several different ways; use repetition.

Dear Lord,
let me listen carefully to
my parents, to my teachers, and
to You. When I listen, I learn.
Let me become a better listener
today than I was yesterday, and
let me become an even better
listener tomorrow.

Amen

8

Knowing Right
from Wrong . . .
and Doing It!

Praise the LORD! Happy are those
who respect the LORD,
who want what he commands.

Psalm 112:1 NCV

If you're old enough to know right from wrong, then you're old enough to do something about it. In other words, you should always try to do the right thing, and you should also do your very best not to do the wrong thing.

The more self-control you have, the easier it is to do the right thing. Why? Because, when you learn to think first and do things next, you avoid lots of silly mistakes. So here's great advice: first, slow down long enough to figure out the right thing to do—and then do it. You'll make yourself happy, and you'll make lots of other people happy, too.

When in doubt, ask mom or dad: If you're not sure whether something is right or wrong, ask your parents before you do it!

WOW
Obedience to God is our job.
Elisabeth Elliot

Parent Tip

Listen with your ears, your eyes, and your heart. And remember: wise parents pay careful attention to the things their children don't say.

Dear Lord,
when I'm tempted to do
the wrong thing, help me to
slow down and to think about
my behavior. And then,
help me to know what's right
and to do what's right.

Amen

When in Doubt, Pray about It

Always be happy. Never stop praying.
Give thanks whatever happens.
That is what God wants for you
in Christ Jesus.

1 Thessalonians 5:16-18 ICB

Do you really want to become a more patient person? Then pray about it. Would you like to learn how to use better self-control? Then pray about it. If you are upset, pray about it. If there is something you're worried about, ask God to comfort you. And as you pray more, you'll discover that God is always near and that He's always ready to hear from you. So don't worry about things; pray about them. God is waiting . . . and listening!

Pray early and often: One way to make sure that your heart is in tune with God is to pray often. The more you talk to God, the more He will talk to you.

WOW
Prayer is never the least we can do;
it is always the most!

A. W. Tozer

Parent Tip

Sometimes, the answer to prayer is "No." God doesn't grant all of our requests, nor should He. We must help our children understand that our prayers are answered by a sovereign, all-knowing God, and that we must trust His answers.

Dear Lord,
help me remember
the importance of prayer.
You always hear my prayers, God;
let me always pray them!

Amen

10
Parents Can Help

Honor your father and your mother.

Exodus 20:12 ICB

Whenever you want to get better at something, you should always be willing to let your parents help out in any way they can. After all, your parents want you to become the very best person you can be. So, if you want to become better at controlling your own behavior, ask your parents to help. How can they help out? By reminding you to slow down and think about things before you do them—not after. It's as simple as that.

Calm down . . . sooner rather than later!
If you're angry with a friend or family member, don't blurt out something unkind. If you can't say anything nice, go to your room and don't come out until you can.

WOW

Examine yourselves—ask, each of you,
"Have I been a good brother? . . . son?
. . . husband? . . . father? . . . servant?"

Charles Kingsley

Parent Tip

Hey Mom and Dad, how do you treat *your* parents? If you're lucky enough to have parents who are living, remember that the way you treat them is the way you're training your kids to treat you.

PRAY TiME

Dear Lord,
You have given me a family
that cares for me and loves me.
Thank You. Let me love
everybody in my family,
even when they're not perfect.
And let me always be thankful
that my family loves me even
when I'm not perfect.

Amen

11

Slowing Down Long Enough to Listen

Wise people can also listen and learn.

Proverbs 1:5 NCV

When God made you, He gave you two ears and one mouth for a very good reason: you can learn at least twice as much by listening as you can by talking. That's why it's usually better to listen first and talk second. But when you're frustrated or tired, it's easy to speak first and think later.

A big part of growing up is learning how to slow down long enough to listen to the things that people have to say. So the next time you're tempted to turn off your ears and tune up your mouth, stop, listen, and think. After all, God gave you two wonderful ears for a very good reason: to use them.

Listening shows you care: When you listen to the things other people have to say, it shows that you care about their message and about them. Listening carefully is not just the courteous thing to do, it's also the kind thing to do.

WOW
People don't care how much you know until they know how much you care.
Zig Ziglar

Listen first, then speak: For most parents, the temptation to lecture is great; it takes conscious effort to hold one's tongue until one's ears are fully engaged. When a parent is able to do so, his or her efforts are usually rewarded.

59

Dear Lord,
I have lots to learn. Help me
to watch, to listen, to think,
and to learn, every day
of my life.

Amen

12
The Rewards of Self-control

So prepare your minds for service and have self-control.

1 Peter 1:13 NCV

Who needs to learn more about self-control? You do! Why? Well, for one thing, you'll discover that good things happen to people (like you) who are wise enough to think ahead and smart enough to look before they leap.

Whether you're at home or at school, you'll learn that the best rewards go to the kids who control their behavior—not to the people who let their behaviors control them!

Use the **Golden Rule** to help you decide what to say and how to behave: Treat people like you want to be treated!

WOW
Nobody is good by accident.
No man ever became holy by chance.
C. H. Spurgeon

Be disciplined in your own approach to life: You can't teach it if you won't live it.

Dear Lord,
You have given me so many
blessings, and You want to give
me even more. Thank You.
Here's how I will show my
thanks: I will use my talents,
and I will behave myself.

Amen

13

Stop, Look, and Think!

A wise person is patient.

Proverbs 19:11 ICB

The Book of Proverbs tells us that self-control and patience are very good things to have. But for most of us, self-control and patience can also be very hard things to learn.

Are you having trouble being patient? And are you having trouble slowing down long enough to think before you act? If so, remember that self-control takes practice, and lots of it, so keep trying. And if you make a mistake, don't be too upset. After all, if you're going to be a really patient person, you shouldn't just be patient with others; you should also be patient with yourself.

Stop, think, then speak: If you want to make your words useful instead of hurtful, don't open your mouth until you've turned on your brain!

WOW
Teach us, O Lord, the disciplines
of patience, for to wait is often
harder than to work.

Peter Marshall

Words, words, words . . . are important, important, important! And, some of the most important words you will ever speak are the ones that your children hear. So whether or not you are talking *directly* to your kids, choose your words carefully.

PRAY TIME

Dear Lord,
let me be patient with other
people's mistakes. And let me
be patient with my own. I know
that I still have so many things
to learn. I won't stop learning,
I won't give up, and I won't stop
growing up. Every day, I will do
my best to become a little bit
more like the person You
intend for me to be.

Amen

14

You Don't Have to Go Along with the Crowd

Do you think I am trying to make people accept me? No, God is the One I am trying to please. Am I trying to please people? If I still wanted to please people, I would not be a servant of Christ.

Galatians 1:10 NCV

It happens to all of us at one time or another: a friend asks us to do something that we think is wrong. What should we do? Should we try to please our friend by doing something bad? No way! It's not worth it!

Trying to please our friends is okay. What's not okay is misbehaving in order to do so.

Do you have a friend who encourages you to misbehave? Hopefully you don't have any friends like that. But if you do, say "No, NO, NOOOOOO!" And what if your friend threatens to break up the friendship? Let him! Friendships like that just aren't worth it.

Face facts: Since you can't please everybody, you're better off trying to please the people who are trying to help you become a better person, not the people who are encouraging you to misbehave!

WOW
True friends will always lift you higher and challenge you to walk in a manner pleasing to our Lord.

Lisa Bevere

Remind your child . . . that it's more important to be respected than to be liked.

Dear Lord,
there's a right way and a wrong way to do things. Let me do what's right and keep doing what's right every day of my life.

Amen

15

Learning Lessons from Our Mistakes . . . the First Time

A wise person pays attention to correction
that will improve his life.

Proverbs 15:31 ICB

Do you ever make mistakes? Of course you do . . . everybody does. And when you make a mistake, it's not so terrible if you learn something. Why should you try to learn from your mistakes? So you won't make the very same mistakes again.

When you have done things that you regret, you should apologize, you should clean up the mess you've made, you should learn from your mistakes, and—last but not least—you should forgive yourself. Mistakes happen . . . it's simply a fact of life, and it's simply a part of growing up. So don't be too hard on yourself, especially if you've learned something along the way.

Made a mistake? Ask for forgiveness? If you've broken one of God's rules, you can always ask Him for His forgiveness. And He will always give it!

WOW

God is able to take mistakes, when they are committed to Him, and make of them something for our good and for His glory.

Ruth Bell Graham

When angels fall . . . Even your own angelic child may make a mistake on occasion. When the unlikely happens, help your boy or girl understand why the behavior is wrong and how to prevent it in the future.

PRAY TIME

Dear Lord,
sometimes I make mistakes.
When I do, help me learn
something, help me forgive
myself, and help me become
a smarter person today
than I was yesterday.

Amen

16
What the Bible Says

Your word is like a lamp for my feet
and a light for my way.

Psalm 119:105 ICB

What book contains everything that God has to say about self-control? The Bible, of course. If you read the Bible every day, you'll soon be convinced that self-control is very important to God. And, since doing the right thing (and the smart thing) is important to your Father in heaven, it should be important to you, too.

The Bible is the most important book you'll ever own. It's God's Holy Word. Read it every day, and follow its instructions. When you do, you'll be safe now and forever.

KID TIP

Read the Bible? Every day!: Try to read your Bible with your parents every day. If they forget, remind them!

WOW
The Bible is God's Word, given to us by God Himself so we can know Him and His will for our lives.

Billy Graham

Parent Tip

It's up to us: Our children will learn about Jesus at church and, in some cases, at school. But, the ultimate responsibility for religious teachings should never be delegated to institutions outside the home. As parents, we must teach our children about the love and grace of Jesus Christ by our words and by our actions.

Dear Lord,
the Bible is Your gift to me.
Let me use it, let me trust it,
and let me obey it, today
and every day that I live.

Amen

17

When in Doubt, Slow Down

Be still, and know that I am God . . . .

✿ ✿ ✿

Psalm 46:10 NKJV

Maybe you're one of those people who try to do everything fast, faster, or fastest! If so, maybe you sometimes do things before you think about the consequences of your actions. If that's the case, it's probably a good idea to slow down a little bit so you can think before you act. When you do, you'll soon discover the value of thinking carefully about things before you get started. And while you're at it, it's probably a good idea to think before you speak, too. After all, you'll never have to apologize for something that you didn't say.

Got questions? If you're faced with too many questions and too few answers, slow down, and talk to your parents. When you do, you'll discover that your parents probably have more answers than you have questions.

WOW
You can always go to God with your
questions. You may not find all
the answers, but in finding God,
you know the One who does.
Max Lucado

Put the brakes on impulsive behavior . . . theirs and yours!

Dear Lord,
sometimes this world can be
a puzzling place. When I am
unsure what to do, let me be
quick to learn from my parents,
and let me be quick to
learn from You.

Amen

18

Homework

Remember what you are taught.
And listen carefully to words
of knowledge.

Proverbs 23:12 ICB

Sooner or later, you'll start getting homework, and when that day comes, you'd better be ready because that's when you'll really need lots of self-control! Usually, homework isn't hard to do, but it takes time. And sometimes, you would rather be doing other things (like playing outside or watching TV). But, when you put off our homework until the last possible minute, we make it hard on ourselves.

Instead of putting off your homework, do it first. Then, you'll have the rest of your time to have fun—and you won't have to worry about all that homework.

The habit of putting things off . . . is a habit that you're better off without.

WOW
Not now becomes never.
Martin Luther

Teach by example: Whatever "it" is, do it now. When you do, you'll demonstrate to your child the value of self-discipline.

Dear Lord,
You have given me a wonderful
gift: time here on earth.
Let me use it wisely today
and every day that I live.

Amen

19

Quiet Please

In quietness and confidence
shall be your strength.

Isaiah 30:15 NKJV

Have you learned how to sit quietly and listen to your parents and your teachers? Have you learned how to listen respectfully—with your ears open wide and your mouth closed tight? If so, give yourself a big pat on the back (or if you can't reach way back there, ask your mom or dad to do it for you!).

An important part of learning self-control is learning how to be quiet when you're supposed to be quiet. It isn't always easy, but the sooner you learn how to sit quietly and behave respectfully, the better. So you might as well start today.

And when you speak, be respectful to everybody, starting with parents, grandparents, teachers, and adults . . . but don't stop there. Be respectful of everybody, including yourself!

WOW
Sometimes, we must be quiet so
we can hear God say all that He wants
to say to us in our hearts.
Charles Swindoll

Silence is okay: Sometimes, just being there is enough. If you're not sure what to say, it's okay to say nothing.

Dear Lord,
let me listen respectfully to
my parents, to my teachers,
and to You. I have much to learn.
Let me learn as much as I can
as soon as I can, and let me
be a good example for other
people to follow.

Amen

20

Don't Give Up

We must not become tired of doing good.

Galatians 6:2 ICB

If you're having trouble learning how to control your actions or your emotions, you're not alone! Most people have problems with self-control from time to time, so don't be discouraged. Just remember that self-control requires practice and lots of it. So if you're a little discouraged, don't give up. Just keep working on improving your self-control until you get better at it. . . . and if you keep trying, you can be sure that sooner or later, you will get better at it.

Everybody is a VIP: VIP means "Very Important Person." To God, everybody is a VIP, and we should treat every person with dignity, patience, and respect.

WOW
We do the works, but God works in us in helping us do the works.

St. Augustine

Parent Tip

Self-control is as self-control does: Your children will learn about self-control by watching you (not by listening to you!). It's a scary thought, of course, but with God's help, you're up to the task!

PRAY TiME

Dear Lord,
help me to make Your world
a better place. I can't fix all
the world's troubles, but I can
help make things better with
kind words, good deeds,
and sincere prayers. Let my
actions and my prayers be
pleasing to You, Lord,
now and forever.

Amen

21

Parents Are Smarter Than You Think

My child, listen to your father's teaching.
And do not forget your mother's advice.

Proverbs 1:8 ICB

Do you listen carefully to the things your parents tell you? You should. Your parents want the very best for you. They want you to be happy and healthy; they want you to be smart and to do smart things. Your parents have much to teach you, and you have much to learn. So listen carefully to the things your mom and dad have to say. And ask lots of questions. When you do, you'll soon discover that your parents have lots of answers . . . lots of very good answers.

KiD TiP

Talking versus *really* talking: Don't be too embarrassed or too fearful to tell your parents what you're really thinking about. They understand more than you think they do!

WOW
The home should be a school where
life's basic lessons are taught.
Billy Graham

Parent Tip

Some choices WE must make: Of course we want to give our children room to grow, but some decisions must be reserved for the wisest men and women of the family (us). Those choices include matters of personal health and safety and the core principles by which we, as parents, intend to raise our families.

Dear Lord,
let me be respectful of
all people, starting with my
family and friends. And, let me
share the love that I feel in
my heart with them . . .
and with You!

Amen

No More Tantrums

Do not become angry easily.
Anger will not help you live a good life
as God wants.

James 1:19 ICB

Temper tantrums are one of the silliest ways to lose self-control. Why? Because when we lose our temper, we say things that we shouldn't say, and we do things that we shouldn't do. And to make matters worse, once the tantrum is over, we usually feel embarrassed or worse. Too bad!

The Bible tells us that it is usually foolish to become angry and that it is wise to remain calm. That's why we should learn to control our tempers before our tempers control us.

KID TIP

Think carefully . . . make that very carefully! If you're a little angry, think carefully before you speak. If you're very angry, think very carefully. Otherwise, you might say something mean that you'll be sorry you said.

WOW
When you strike out in anger,
you may miss the other person,
but you will always hit yourself.
Jim Gallery

Parent Tip

Keeping your cool 101: When your child becomes upset, you'll be tempted to become upset, too. Resist that temptation. Remember that in a house full of kids and grownups, you're the grown-up. And it's up to you to remain calm even when other, less mature members of the family can't.

Dear Lord,
help me to turn away from
angry thoughts and angry people.
Help me always to use Jesus
as my guide for life, and let me
trust His promises today
and forever.

Amen

23

Being an Example to Others

You are the light that gives light to the world. In the same way, you should be a light for other people. Live so that they will see the good things you do and will praise your Father in heaven.

❋ ❋ ❋

Matthew 5:14,16 NCV

What kind of example are you? Are you the kind of person who shows other people what it means to be well behaved? And, are you learning to use more and more self-control? Hopefully so!!!

Whether you realize it or not, you're an example to your friends and family members. So today, be a good example for others to follow. Because God needs people (like you) who are willing to behave themselves as God intends. And that's exactly the kind of example you should try to be.

Look around! Someone very near you may need a helping hand or a kind word, so keep your eyes open, and look for people who need your help, whether at home, at church, or at school.

WOW
One of the best ways to witness
to family, friends, and neighbors is
to let them see the difference
Jesus has made in your life.
Anne Graham Lotz

Teaching values: Your children will learn about life from many sources; the most important source can and should be you. But remember that the lectures you give are never as important as the ones you live. So teach the importance of self-control every day and, if necessary, use words.

Dear Lord,
make me a worthy example
to my family and friends.
And, let my words and my deeds
serve as a testimony to the
changes You have made in my
life. Let me praise You, Father,
by following in the footsteps
of Your Son, and let others see
Him through me.

Amen

24

Listen . . . and Obey

Teach me, O Lord, the way of Your statutes, and I shall keep it to the end. Give me understanding, and I shall keep Your law; indeed, I shall observe it with my whole heart.

✻ ✻ ✻

Psalm 119:33-34 NKJV

When you learn to control your actions and your words, you will find it easier to obey your parents, your teachers, and your Father in heaven. Why? Because in order to be an obedient person, you must first learn how to control yourself—otherwise, you won't be able to obey very well, even when you want to.

When you learn the importance of obedience, you'll soon discover that good things happen when you behave yourself. And the sooner you learn to listen and obey, the sooner those good things will start happening.

KiD TiP

Obeying God? Yes Sir! What about the rules you learn in the Bible? Well, those aren't just any old rules—they're God's rules. And you should behave—and obey—accordingly.

WOW
Let us trust God's promises
and obey His commandments.
John Calvin

Parent Tip

See as much as you can; correct as much as you should: Teaching your child the importance of disciplined behavior requires an observing eye and a patient heart. You should expect your child to be well behaved, but you should not expect your child to be perfect. In fact, an important part of parenting is knowing what to overlook and when to overlook it.

Dear Lord,
You know what's best for me.
I will study Your Word
and obey Your teachings
this day and forever.

Amen

25

If You're Not Sure What to Do

I will instruct you and teach you in the way you should go; I will guide you with My eye.

❈❈❈

Psalm 32:8 NKJV

When you're not sure whether something is right or wrong, ask yourself a simple question: "How would Jesus behave if He were here?" The answer to that question will tell you what to do.

Jesus was perfect, but we are not. Still, we must try as hard as we can to do the best that we can. When we do, we will love others, just as Christ loves us.

When in doubt: Do the thing that you think Jesus would do. And, of course, don't do something if you think that He wouldn't do it.

WOW
There is something incredibly comforting about knowing that the Creator is in control of your life.

Lisa Whelchel

Want them to know what Jesus would do? Then teach them what Jesus did!

Dear Lord,
even when I don't understand
why things happen, I will trust
You. Even when I am confused or
worried, I will trust You. There
are many things that I cannot
do, Lord, and there are many
things that I cannot understand.
But one thing I can do is to trust
You always. And I will.

Amen

26

Safety First

Innocent people will be kept safe.
But those who are dishonest
will suddenly be ruined.

Proverbs 28:18 ICB

Self-control and safety go hand in hand. Why? Because a big part of self-control is looking around and thinking things through before you do something that you might regret later.

Remember the saying "Look before you leap!"? Well, if you want to live safely and happily, you should look very carefully before you decide whether or not to leap. After all, it's easy to leap, but once you're in the middle of your jump, it's too late to leap back!

Don't complain about safety: Whether it's a fire drill at school or wearing seat belts in the family car, don't whine, complain, or resist. When grown-ups are trying to keep you safe, your job is to help them do it!

WOW
In God's faithfulness lies eternal security.
Corrie ten Boom

Thinking ahead for your child: As a responsible parent, it's up to you to be your family's safety expert. Impulsive kids, left to their own devices, tend to get themselves into dangerous situations; responsible adults, however, don't leave kids to their own devices.

Dear Lord,
You protect me; help me
to learn how to protect myself.
Help me to slow down, to think
ahead, and to look before
I leap. You are concerned with
my safety, Lord. Help me to
be concerned with it, too.

Amen

27

When Nobody Is Around

Good people will be guided by honesty;
dishonesty will destroy those
who are not trustworthy.

❋ ❋ ❋

Proverbs 11:3 NCV

Even when nobody's watching, God is. And He knows whether you've done the right thing or the wrong thing. So if you're tempted to misbehave when nobody is looking, remember this: There is never a time when "nobody's watching." Somebody is always watching over you—and that Somebody, of course, is your Father in heaven. Don't let Him down!

Want something? Ask, don't take! It's okay to ask. It's not okay to take!

WOW
God doesn't expect you to be perfect, but he does insist on complete honesty.
Rick Warren

Parent Tip

Displaying integrity in matters both great and small: Right is right and wrong is wrong whether the issue appears large or inconsequential. And when it comes to issues of integrity, you are a 24-hour-a-day example to your child, so be on guard.

Dear Lord,
help me to behave myself like
a good Christian! Let me keep
Christ in my heart, and let me
put the devil in his place:
far away from me!

Amen

28

What It Means to Be Wise

Wisdom begins with respect for the LORD.

Proverbs 9:10 ICB

If you look in a dictionary, you'll see that the word *wisdom* means "using good judgment, and knowing what is true." But there's more: it's not just enough to know what's right; if you really want to become a wise person, you must also do what's right.

A big part of "doing what's right" is learning self-control . . . and the best day to start learning self-control is this one!

Learning about Jesus: Start learning about Jesus, and keep learning about Him as long as you live. His story never grows old, and His teachings never fail.

WOW
If you lack knowledge, go to school.
If you lack wisdom,
get on your knees and pray.
Vance Havner

Parent Tip

Stress the importance of learning: Some families stress the importance of education more than other families. Make yours a home in which the importance of education is clearly a high priority.

Dear Lord,
I trust Your wisdom. The most important wisdom is Yours, and the most important truth is Yours. Today, I will show my respect for You by obeying Your commandments.

Amen

29

You'll Be Happier

Happy is the person who . . .
loves what the LORD commands.

❋❋❋

Psalm 112:1 ICB

Do you want to be happy? Here are some things you should do: Love God and His Son, Jesus; obey the Golden Rule; learn how to control yourself, and always try to do what you think is right. When you do these things, you'll discover that happiness goes hand in hand with good behavior.

The happiest people do not misbehave; the happiest people are not cruel or thoughtless. The happiest people don't say unkind things. The happiest people are those who love God and follow his rules— starting, of course, with the Golden one.

Better self-control can help make you happy: The better you behave, the more fun you'll have. And don't let anybody try to tell you otherwise.

WOW
Joy is the serious business of heaven.
C. S. Lewis

Parent Tip

Parents make the best encouragers! You're not just your children's parents, you're also their biggest fans. Make sure they know it.

Dear Lord,
I am thankful for all
the blessings You have given me.
Let me be a happy Christian,
Father, as I share Your joy
with friends, with family,
and with the world.

Amen

30

Because It's What God Wants

"Not My will, but Yours, be done."

Luke 22:42 NKJV

How much does God love you? He loves you so much that He sent His Son Jesus to come to this earth for you! And, when you accept Jesus into your heart, God gives you a gift that is more precious than gold: that gift is called "eternal life," which means that you will live forever with God in heaven!

God's love is bigger and more powerful than anybody can imagine, but it is very real. So do yourself a favor right now: accept God's love with open arms and welcome His Son Jesus into your heart. When you do, your life will be changed today, tomorrow, and forever.

Self-control every day: Self-control should be part of our lives every day, not just on the days when we feel good. God loves us every day, and we should obey Him every day. And remember: good behavior starts with you, but if you're a good example to others, it won't end there!

WOW
True faith commits us to obedience.
A. W. Tozer

He's watching us, too. Of course we know that God watches over us, but we must also make certain that our children know that we know. And, we must behave in ways that let our children know that we know that He knows. Whew!

Dear Lord,
thank You for watching over me.
Help me understand what's
right and do what's right,
today and always.

Amen

31
Your Friend Forever

And Jesus said to them, "I am the bread of life. He who comes to Me shall never hunger, and he who believes in Me shall never thirst."

John 6:35 NKJV

There's an old song that says, "What a friend we have in Jesus." Those words are certainly true! When you invite Him into your heart, Jesus will be your friend forever. If you make mistakes, He'll still be your friend. If you behave badly, He'll still love you. If you feel sorry or sad, He can help you feel better if you ask Him to.

Jesus wants you to have a happy, healthy life. He wants you to behave yourself, and He wants you to take care of yourself. And now, it's up to you to do your best to live up to the hopes and dreams of your very best friend: Jesus.

Jesus loves me, this I know . . . but how much? Here's how much: Jesus loves you so much that He gave His life so that you might live forever with Him in heaven. And how can you repay Christ's love? By accepting Him into your heart and by obeying His rules. When you do, He will love you and bless you today, tomorrow, and forever.

WOW

Tell me the story of Jesus. Write on my heart every word. Tell me the story most precious, sweetest that ever was heard.

Fanny Crosby

Parent Tip

Don't be embarrassed to discuss your faith: You need not have attended seminary to have worthwhile opinions about your faith. Express those opinions, especially to your children; your kids need to know where you stand.

139

Dear Lord,
I am only here on this earth
for a while. But, because of
Your Son Jesus, I will be with
You forever in heaven. Let me
share that Good News
with my family and friends.

Amen

Bible Verses to Memorize

Patience is better
than strength.

Proverbs 16:32 ICB

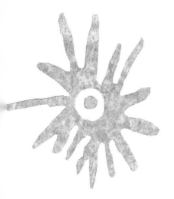

Trust the LORD with
all your heart. Don't depend
on your own understanding.
Remember the Lord in
everything you do. And
he will give you success.

Proverbs 3:5-6 ICB

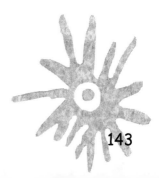

Draw near to God,
and He will
draw near to you.

❋ ❋ ❋

James 4:8 HCSB

Self-control

I have come that they
may have life, and that
they may have it
more abundantly.

※ ※ ※

John 10:10 NKJV

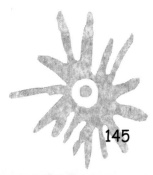

Wisdom begins with
respect for the LORD.

Proverbs 9:10 ICB

Do to others what you want them to do to you.

❋ ❋ ❋

Matthew 7:12 NCV

Now these three remain:
faith, hope, and love.
But the greatest of these
is love.

1 Corinthians 13:13 HCSB

We love Him because
He first loved us.

❄ ❄ ❄

1 John 4:19 NKJV

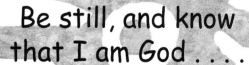

Be still, and know
that I am God . . . .

Psalm 46:10 KJV

Jesus said to him,
"You shall love the LORD your
God with all your heart,
with all your soul, and with
all your mind. This is
the first and great
commandment. And
the second is like it:
'You shall love your neighbor
as yourself."

Matthew 22:37-39 NKJV

For the LORD is good;
His mercy is everlasting,
and His truth endures
to all generations.

❈ ❈ ❈

Psalm 100:5 NKJV

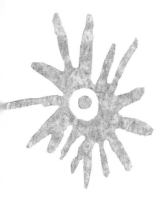

The LORD is my shepherd;
I shall not want. He makes
me to lie down in green
pastures; He leads me
beside the still waters.
He restores my soul.

❊ ❊ ❊

Psalm 23:1-3 NKJV

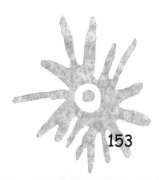

I am able to do
all things through Him
who strengthens me.

Philippians 4:13 HCSB

For God so loved the world,
that he gave his only
begotten Son, that
whosoever believeth in
him should not perish,
but have everlasting life.

❀ ❀ ❀

John 3:16 KJV

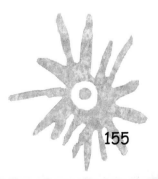

This is the day that the LORD has made. Let us rejoice and be glad today!

❀ ❀ ❀

Psalm 118:24 ICB

Let not your heart be troubled; you believe in God, believe also in Me.

❋ ❋ ❋

John 14:1 NKJV

Little Book Devotions help parents and children discuss important Biblical themes by relating those themes to the challenges of everyday life. These books are intended to be read *by* parents *to* children. Current titles include:

Little Book Devotions Honesty
Little Book Devotions Kindness
Little Book Devotions Patience
Little Book Devotions Forgiveness
Little Book Devotions Self-Control
Little Book Devotions Sharing

Additional titles are coming soon.

Little Book Devotions are available in LifeWay Christian Stores.